INSIDE
TORNADOES

By Mary Kay Carson

STERLING

STERLING and the distinctive Sterling logo are registered trademarks
of Sterling Publishing Co., Inc.

Library of Congress Cataloging-in-Publication Data Available
Lot#:
2 4 6 8 10 9 7 5 3 1
05/10
Published by Sterling Publishing Co., Inc.
387 Park Avenue South, New York, NY 10016
© 2010 by Mary Kay Carson
Distributed in Canada by Sterling Publishing
c/o Canadian Manda Group, 165 Dufferin Street
Toronto, Ontario, Canada M6K 3H6
Distributed in the United Kingdom by GMC Distribution Services
Castle Place, 166 High Street, Lewes, East Sussex, England BN7 1XU
Distributed in Australia by Capricorn Link (Australia) Pty. Ltd.
P.O. Box 704, Windsor, NSW 2756, Australia

Printed in China
All rights reserved.

Sterling ISBN 978-1-4027-5879-9 (hardcover)
978-1-4027-7781-3 (flexibound)

For information about custom editions, special sales, premium and
corporate purchases, please contact Sterling Special Sales
Department at 800-805-5489 or specialsales@sterlingpublishing.com.

Designed by Celia Fuller.

IMAGE CREDITS: AP Photo/The Daily Oklahoman/Paul Hellstern: 30–31; AP Photo/Charlie Neibergall: 41 (foreground); AP Photo/LM Otero: 31 (bottom foreground); AP Photo/Steve Pyle: 28 (foreground); AP Photo/University of Chicago: 25; © Roberto Giudici/Colbel Photo Agency: 35–36; © Bettmann/Corbis: 26 (background and foreground), 27, 29 (top background); © Jim Edds/Corbis: 1, 18 (left); © Warren Faidley/Corbis: 18 (right); © Andrew Fox/Corbis: 23 (top); © Douglas Keister/Corbis: 17 (top right); © Eric Nguyen/Corbis: 2–3, 13 (top right); © Jim Reed/Corbis: 17 (left), 19 (left); © Reuters/CORBIS: 10-11 (background), 24 (top); © VALENTIN FLAURAUD/Reuters/Corbis: 44; © Dave Kaup/Reuters/Corbis: 24 (bottom); © Mike Hollingshead/Science Faction/Corbis: 4/9; © Mike Theiss/Ultimate Chase/Corbis: 24 (middle), 33 (background), back flap; © Visuals Unlimited/Corbis: 20; Michael Raphael/FEMA: 23 (middle); GeoEye satellite image: 37; © iStockphoto.com/"Josh Banks": 12 (background), 13 (background), 14 (background), 15 (background), back cover (bottom); © iStockphoto.com/"Tammy Bryngelson": 23–24; © iStockphoto.com/"Sonja Foos": 47; © iStockphoto.com/"sebastian-julian": 7–8 (background); © iStockphoto.com/"Stefan Klein": 46; © iStockphoto.com/"Jakub Marad": 19 (bottom right); © iStockphoto.com/"Sean Martin": 45; © iStockphoto.com/"Bart Sadowski": 5–6 (background); © iStockphoto.com/"Roel Smart": 28 (bottom background), 29 (bottom background), 31 (bottom background), 34 (bottom), 41 (bottom background); © iStockphoto.com/"Clint Spencer": 17 (bottom right); Maps and Diagrams by Joe LeMonnier: 5–6 (foreground), 7 (foreground), 9 (foreground), 11 (foreground), 12 (foreground), 13 (foreground), 14 (top and bottom foreground), 15 (foreground), 16/21, 22, 28 (top), 29 (top foreground), 31 (top), 34 (top), 39 (right); Created by the National Center for Supercomputing Applications (NCSA) at the University of Illinois at Urbana-Champaign. © Copyright 2006 The Board of Trustees of the University of Illinois: 42; National Oceanic and Atmospheric Administration (NOAA): 39 (left); NOAA Photo Library, Weather Service Collection: 29 (foreground); Herbert Stein: 38, 40, back cover (top); U.S. Department of Agriculture, Farm Service Agency, National Agriculture Imagery Program (NAIP), 2006: 32; WeatherTAP.com: 33 (foreground); Front cover art: © Reuters/CORBIS

Contents

How to Read This Book

This book is different from most you've read. Many of its pages fold out—or flip up! To know where to read next, follow arrows like these ◈ and look for page numbers like these 🌀 to help you find your place. Happy exploring!

Severe T-Storms

A severe thunderstorm has at least one of the following: winds faster than 58 miles per hour, or mph, (93 kilometers per hour, or km/h); hail larger than ¾-inch (2cm) across; or tornadoes.

Where in the United States Do Tornadoes Happen?

Most U.S. tornadoes happen in eith thunderstorm-soaked Florida or in the Gre Plains. The most violent and destructi kinds of tornadoes—F-5s—are marked wi dots on the map. While Florida's tornado are usually weak, those in the middle the country are often strong. That's why t Midwest is called Tornado Alley!

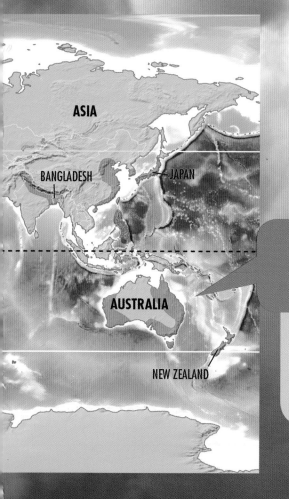

ASIA

BANGLADESH

JAPAN

AUSTRALIA

NEW ZEALAND

Twisters Down Under

Most Australian and other Southern Hemisphere tornadoes rotate clockwise. U.S. and other Northern Hemisphere tornadoes usually spin counterclockwise.

Where and When Do Tornadoes Happen?

It's possible for any thunderstorm anywhere to make a tornado—at any time. But the conditions have to be just right. Certain parts of the world get most of the tornadoes, or twisters. Season and time of day can increase the odds, too. Tornadoes tend to happen when and where strong thunderstorms are most common.

Where in the World Do Tornadoes Happen?

Tornadoes twist across every continent except Antarctica. As the map shows, most happen about halfway between the South Pole and the equator and the North Pole and the equator. What places outside of North America see lots of twister action? Northern Europe, western Asia, Bangladesh, Japan, Australia, and New Zealand.

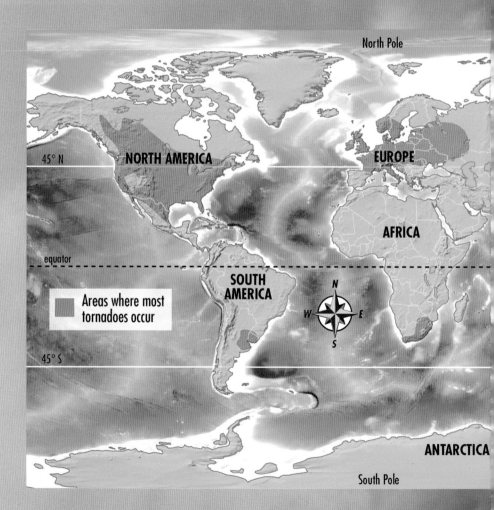

North Pole

45° N

NORTH AMERICA

EUROPE

AFRICA

equator

SOUTH AMERICA

■ Areas where most tornadoes occur

N
W   E
S

45° S

ANTARCTICA

South Pole

Twisted Weather

Springtime thunderstorms on the Great Plains put on an exciting show. Dark clouds roll in, rain falls in buckets, and lightning bolts brighten the night sky for miles. The thunder is so loud you can feel it in your chest—like fireworks. Ka-BOOM!

Some of these spring thunderstorms threaten more than rain and lightning. Severe thunderstorms bring black clouds that spew hail so big it dents car roofs. When the hail stops, the air is eerily still and smells like wet dirt. The super-sized storm isn't over yet. The sky is a spooky greenish-yellow.

Local folks know what a greenish sky means: Watch out for tornadoes. Tornadoes are Earth's most violent storms. All their destructive power is focused into a short-lived burst of spiraling wind.

When the tornado-warning sirens howl, most people head for a basement. But others actually run the wrong way! Tornado-chasing scientists speed toward these dangerous storms. Their trucks are full of weather-measuring gear. These scientists are trying to understand why and how some thunderstorms create tornadoes. Figuring that out will help keep people safer. However, tornadoes haven't given up their secret recipe yet. The chase for the stormy secret goes on.

Why and How Do Tornadoes Happen?

A tornado is unmistakable. You'd recognize one anywhere. It's a whirling dark cone of unpredictable force. What is a tornado exactly? Why—and *how*—do they happen?

A Short, Violent Life

A tornado is a kind of violent windstorm. It's a chunk of fast-spinning air, called a vortex, stretched between a thunderstorm cloud and the ground.

Connecting to the ground is what makes a tornado such a threat. The winds inside a tornado vortex whirl at speeds up to 300 mph (483km/h). No other storm packs this much punch. Tornadoes can level buildings, lift trains off tracks, and toss cars around like toys. Tornado winds are strong enough to turn even a tiny blade of grass into a dangerous missile!

Thousands of tornadoes happen around the world each year. The United States alone averages about 1,200 a year; Canada has approximately 100. Every year, tornadoes kill hundreds of people worldwide. Bangladesh in southern Asia has averaged more than 175 tornado deaths a year in recent decades. Around sixty to seventy people are killed by tornadoes in the United States each year. Many are injured by flying chunks of trees, homes, or whatever else lies in the path of these violent windstorms.

Extremely destructive tornadoes can have winds up to 300 mph (483km/h), be 10 miles (16km) wide, and plow a damaging path at 60 mph (96km/h) for an hour or more. While these kinds of twisters make headlines, they're thankfully rare. Most tornadoes have milder winds, leave paths of damage less than 1,600 feet (488m) wide, and move at a pokey 35 mph (56km/h) or less for only a few minutes.

What makes one tornado a menace and another mild? Their thunderstorm parents do. Thunderstorms create tornadoes when they release energy. Larger parent storms have more energy and can create stronger tornadoes. Want to make a major tornado? Start with a huge supercell thunderstorm. Supercells are the largest, strongest, and longest-lasting thunderstorms on Earth. They bring large hail, dangerous wind bursts, flash floods, lightning—and sometimes tornadoes.

Stormy Start-ups

Tornadogenesis is a word used to describe the way tornadoes form.

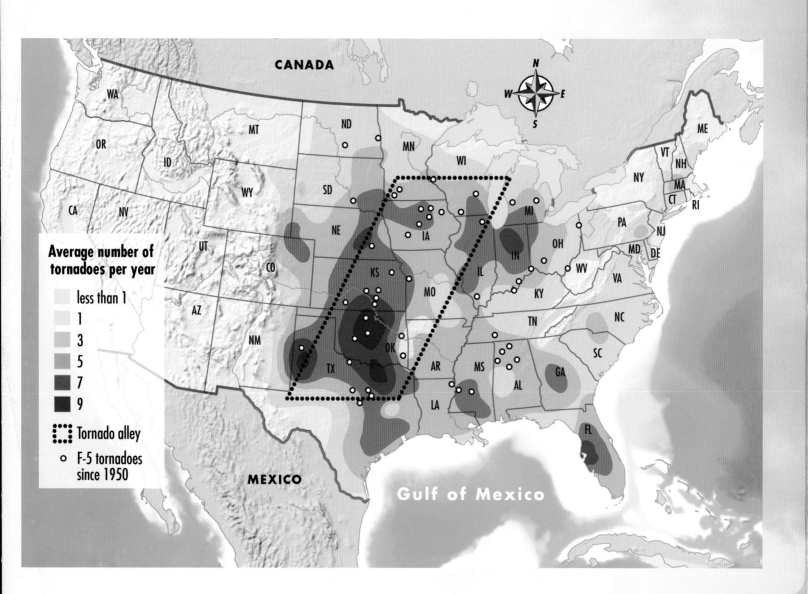

Average number of tornadoes per year

	less than 1
	1
	3
	5
	7
	9

- Tornado alley
- F-5 tornadoes since 1950

CANADA

WA, OR, ID, MT, ND, MN, WI, MI, ME, VT, NH, MA, CT, RI, NY, PA, NJ, CA, NV, WY, SD, NE, IA, IL, IN, OH, MD, DE, UT, CO, KS, MO, KY, WV, VA, AZ, NM, OK, AR, TN, NC, TX, MS, AL, GA, SC, LA, FL

MEXICO

Gulf of Mexico

Short-lived Terror

Most tornadoes don't last longer than ten minutes.

Danger Alley

The U.S. Great Plains has more strong tornadoes than anywhere else on Earth.

Top Ten Tornado States

Rank	Total Tornadoes	Killer Tornadoes	Yearly Tornadoes per 10,000 sq. miles (25,900 sq. km)
1	Texas	Texas	Florida
2	Oklahoma	Oklahoma	Oklahoma
3	Florida	Arkansas	Indiana
4	Kansas	Alabama	Iowa
5	Nebraska	Mississippi	Kansas
6	Iowa	Illinois	Delaware
7	Missouri	Missouri	Louisiana
8	Illinois	Indiana	Mississippi
9	South Dakota	Louisiana	Nebraska
10	Louisiana	Tennessee	Texas

When Do Tornadoes Happen?

J=January
F=February
M=March
A= April
MA=May
JU=June
JUL=July
AU=August
S=September
O=October
N=November
D=December

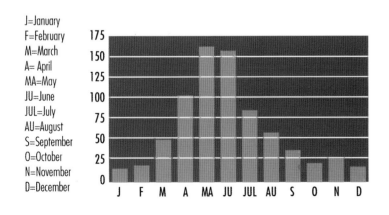

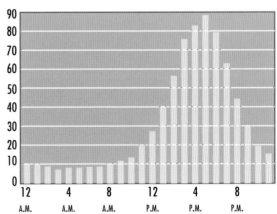

Most tornadoes happen when severe thunderstorms are most common. In the United States, that's warm late afternoons during spring.

Stormy Planet

About 2,000 thunderstorms are happening right now. They're Earth's most common storms, but only a few will create a tornado.

The Right Mix

Ever end up in the wrong place at the worst possible time? This is what happens to the Great Plains each spring. Tornado Alley states lie beneath the violent coming together of atmospheric ingredients that create supercell thunderstorms. Those ingredients come from as far away as the Gulf of Mexico and Canada, but the tornado-making mix happens over prairie states such as Texas, Kansas, Oklahoma, and Nebraska. Here's how:

1 Lots of tropical, humid air hangs over the Gulf of Mexico. As winds blow the warm, moist air inland, it becomes fuel for severe thunderstorms.

2 Cold dry air flows south from chilly Canada. The steep Rocky Mountains help slide the Canadian air toward the plains at a high level.

3 When hot dry air from the desert southwest reaches the moist Gulf air at ground level, the border between them is called a dry line. Up higher, the desert air traps, or caps, the humid Gulf air underneath it. Like a lid on a boiling pot, the dry air keeps the Gulf air from rising into thunderstorms—for a while.

4 Eventually, the Gulf air breaks through the desert air cap. Often it's the battle of air masses at the dry line that weakens the cap. The moist Gulf air bursts free, shooting upward at 100 mph (161km/h), creating a 50,000-foot-tall (15,240m) supercell thunder storm in minutes. The speedy springtime jet stream adds the final ingredient. The high-up current of wind churns the colliding air masses, and the inside of a giant thunderstorm starts to spin—and possibly kick out twisters.

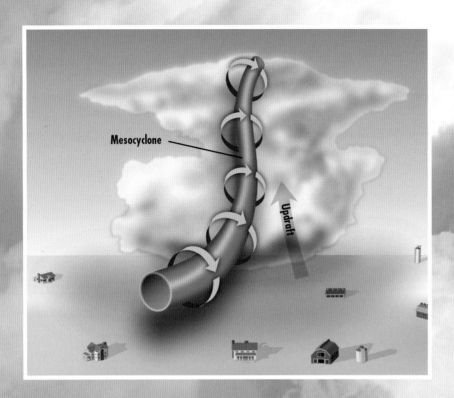

Step 3

Rising air inside the supercell lifts the tube of spinning air upright. The now vertical vortex is called a mesocyclone—a supercell's powerhouse. The 2–6 mile-wide (3–10km) mesocyclone is where a tornado gets its twisting power, too. A mesocyclone is only in the thunderstorm cloud—it's not on the ground.

Step 4

The spinning mesocyclone causes a cloud to drop down below it, like a swelling bump. This is the wall cloud. It's a rain-free, rotating cloud where tornadoes appear.

Step 2

With wind shear spinning a tube of air, the next step toward making a tornado is making a thunderstorm. Warm, moist air slamming into cold, dry air creates a battleground of weather—a front. Hot air rising off the sun-warmed ground punches up through higher cold air. As this warm air cools, its moisture forms clouds. The clouds grow into a thunderstorm as rapidly rising warm air—unstable air—keeps pumping warm, wet air up into the storm. This heat and energy fuels a thunderstorm into a super storm—a supercell thunderstorm. Supercell thunderstorms are big, dangerous, and can last for hours. What's their secret power?

Shear Disaster: Making a Major Twister

Tornado-spewing supercells need four main ingredients: moisture, instability, lift, and wind shear. If the recipe is right, these ingredients can cook up a disastrous tornado.

Step 1
The atmosphere, or air above the ground, has to be right for even the possibility of a tornado. Even before a thunderstorm starts, the atmosphere must make wind shear. Wind shear happens when wind at one height is moving in a different direction or speed than wind at another height. The different winds roll the air between them into a tube of spinning air. Imagine rolling a piece of clay between your sliding hands. As your hands move in different directions, a column of clay is formed. The same effect is at work when wind shear creates a tube of spinning air.

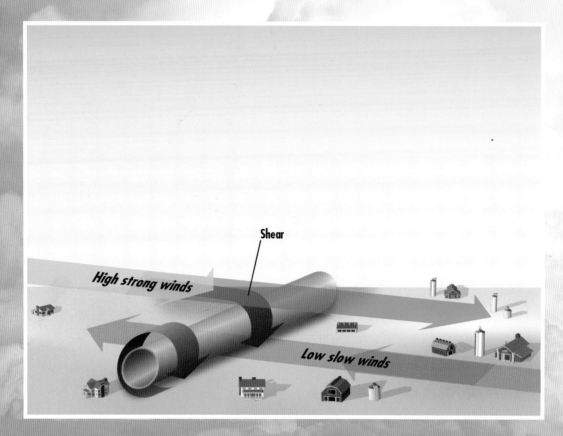

Shear

High strong winds

Low slow winds

A tornado forms between the wall cloud and the ground. Scientists aren't sure yet what triggers this final step. Supercells are full of strong updrafts of hot air and powerful downdrafts of sinking cold air. What triggers a tornado is likely a powerful downward burst of air toward the back of the storm, called the rear flank downdraft (RFD). This RFD wraps around the air between the ground and the wall cloud. Like a tightening belt, it squeezes the rotating air. The squeezed spinning air becomes a tornado.

Rear flank
downdraft
(RFD)

Wall cloud

Tornado

A long, thin **rope tornado** can still be quite powerful.

An **elephant trunk tornado** sways from side to side as it moves

Twister Gallery

Not all tornadoes look the same. Twisters come in different shapes, sizes, and even colors. A tornado gets its color from the dirt, debris, or cloudy air it's twirling.

A **wedge tornado** looks wider than it is tall.

A **stovepipe tornado** has a thick, even, tree-trunk shape.

A **rain-wrap tornado** can be dangerously hidden by the rain around it.

Triggering a Twister

The spinning mesocyclone inside a supercell has plenty of powerful rotating energy. What exactly concentrates a chunk of that whirling power and spins it down to the ground, creating a tornado? "We don't really know for sure," says storm scientist Lou Wicker. Only about 20 percent of supercells make tornadoes. Why some do and others don't is a bit of a modern meteorological mystery. But while no one's sure what triggers that final step, they've got suspects. "The RFD (rear flank downdraft) is a leading candidate," says Wicker.

Right before a twister forms, storm chasers sometimes see a downward rush of air knock a hole in the wall cloud. However, an RFD doesn't always bring a tornado. "That RFD has to curve around and force the air right into the center of the mesocyclone," says Wicker. The whole thing doesn't work if the RFD doesn't connect back into the storm. "To solve the tornado problem, we're going to need a lot more data than we have right now," explains Wicker. More data is why scientists spend each spring chasing tornadoes. They're out there measuring storm ingredients, trying to find the mysterious recipe that triggers a tornado.

Independent Twist

Tornadoes that don't come from a mesocyclone are called nonsupercell tornadoes.

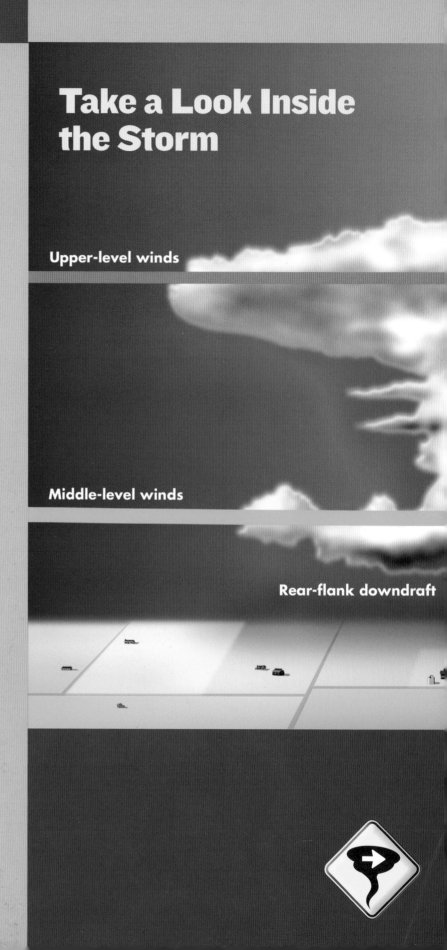

Take a Look Inside the Storm

Upper-level winds

Middle-level winds

Rear-flank downdraft

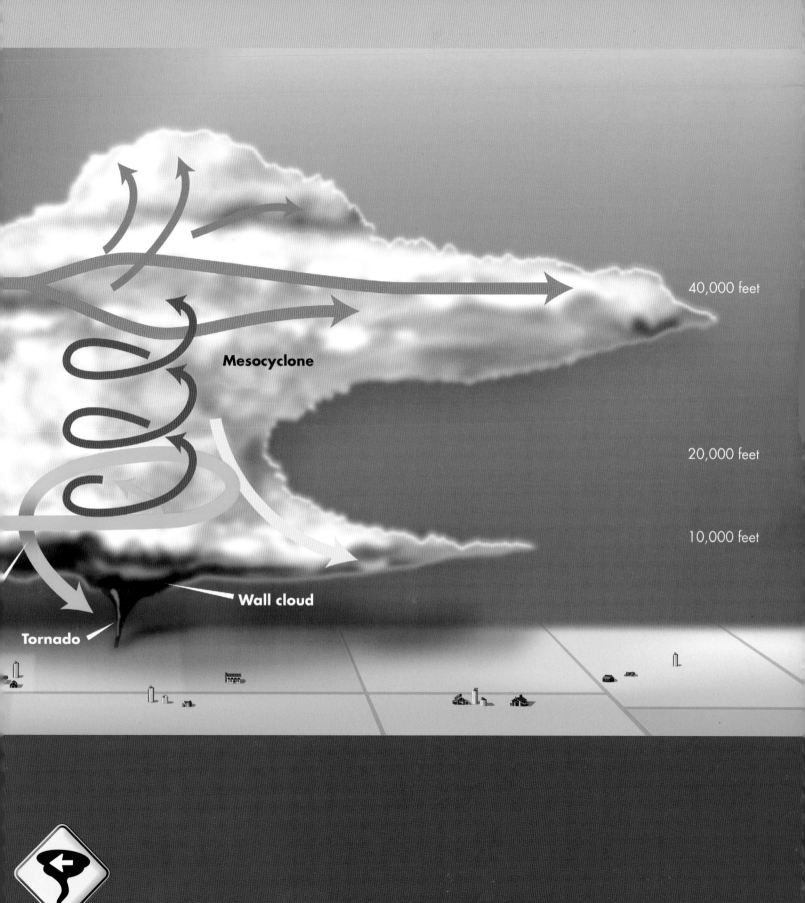

40,000 feet

Mesocyclone

20,000 feet

10,000 feet

Wall cloud

Tornado

Earth's Changing Climate: Are We in for More Tornadoes?

Our planet is warming. Earth's average temperature has been rising for decades. Scientists agree that human-caused pollution from burning coal, oil, and gas are causing the global warming. Rising temperatures change our planet's climate. Scientists predict global climate change will melt icecaps, raise the level of the sea, and bring more extreme weather such as droughts, floods, and storms. Does this mean more tornadoes, too? Let's ask some experts.

"We don't know," says meteorologist Roger Edwards. "It's too soon to say." Warm places—like the tropics—do have more thunderstorms. Warm air rising up into thunderstorms helps the lower atmosphere to get rid of heat. So, the number of thunderstorms may increase with global warming. However, a more thunderstorm-filled world won't necessarily cause more tornadoes. "You might have more really hot, muggy air," explains meteorologist Lou Wicker. "But you may not have as much wind shear to make tornadoes."

More storms don't necessarily mean more tornadoes, agrees Edwards. "For all its power, a tornado needs some very delicate balances of ingredients within any thunderstorm to ever occur," explains Edwards. It's why most thunderstorms don't spin out tornadoes at all. Tornadoes are short-lived, rare weather events.

Edwards reminds us that weather and climate aren't the same thing. Weather is what a particular place is like at a particular time. Climate is the general kind of weather a place usually has. For example, while England's climate might be cool and rainy, the weather in London today could be hot and sunny. Tornadoes are local weather, not climate. Connecting local tornadoes to global temperatures is tough. "It's not much different than trying to connect any particular ten minutes of wind in your backyard to global climate," says Edwards.

A **gustnado** is a kind of weak tornado not created by a supercell. It forms along a thunderstorm's windy gust front.

A rotating bottom of a thunderstorm cloud that doesn't touch the ground is a **funnel cloud**.

When a tornado forms over water, it's called a **waterspout**.

Tornado Activity: Two-Liter Twister

Tornadoes are whirling vortexes of spinning air. Seeing spinning air can be tough, though. Instead, you can make an easy-to-see vortex similar to a tornado, using colored water.

You'll Need:

2 two-liter clear plastic bottles with labels removed
cap for one of the two-liter bottles
duct tape
water
food coloring (any color)

To Do:

1 Fill one of the two-liter bottles about three-quarters full of water.

2 Add a few drops of food coloring to the water in the bottle.

3 Screw the cap back on the bottle and shake to mix in the food coloring. Take off its cap.

4 Place the empty bottle on top of the full bottle, top to top.

5 Use duct tape to securely tape them together, as shown in the diagram.

6 Gently turn the connected bottles upside-down, so the full bottle is now on top. Be careful to hold the bottles firmly so they stay together.

7 Now, act quickly, before water pours through. Hold one hand on the bottom bottle. Use your other hand to swirl the top bottle in a circle. Watch the vortex appear!

8 Repeat steps 6 and 7, swirling the top bottle in the opposite direction. Does it change the vortex?

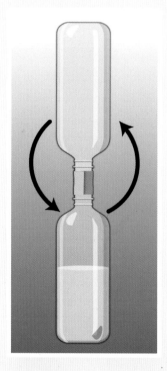 

A vortex of air is invisible. It's whatever is spinning along with air inside the vortex—dust, water, or chunks of a town—that you can see.

HOW BAD WAS IT?
Sizing Up Tornadoes

A tornado isn't easy to measure. Often all anyone sees is the mess a twister leaves behind. That's why scientists use the mess to measure tornadoes. Scientists can tell from the damage done about how fast winds were spiraling inside the storm. Tornadoes are rated from EF-0 to EF-5 on what's called the Enhanced Fujita (EF) Scale. It replaced the old Fujita Scale of F-0 to F-5 in 2007. The Enhanced Fujita scale is a lot like the original Fujita—

both use wind damage to rate tornadoes. After more than three decades studying tornadoes with the Fujita Scale, meteorologists found that the scale often over-rated wind speeds for stronger tornadoes—the kind people are most interested in! The Enhanced Fujita Scale solves this problem by using more details about specific kinds of structures damaged and how they were built. Doing that gives them a more precise rating of tornadoes.

After inventing the Fujita Scale of tornado strength in 1971, Tetsuya Theodore "Ted" Fujita (1920–1998) became known as Mr. Tornado. Ted Fujita simulated tornadoes (like the one shown here) in a laboratory for decades before he saw his first real tornado at age sixty-one.

ENHANCED FUJITA SCALE OF TORNADO INTENSITY

Enhanced Fujita (EF) Rating	Estimated Wind-Gust Speed	Kind of Damage	What the Damage Looks Like
0	65–85 mph (105–137km/h)	**LIGHT DAMAGE:** Causes some damage to shingles on roofs and siding on houses.	
1	86–110 mph (138–177km/h)	**MODERATE DAMAGE:** Lots of roof damage. Winds can uproot trees, tip over mobile homes, and bend flagpoles.	
2	111–135 mph (179–217km/h)	**CONSIDERABLE DAMAGE:** Most mobile homes destroyed. Permanent homes can shift off foundations. Flagpoles collapse. Bark blown off softwood trees.	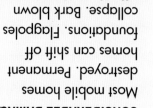

Keeping the Record Straight

Tornadoes that happened before 2007 will still have old F-0 to F-5 Fujita Scale ratings.

3

136–165 mph
(219–266km/h)

SEVERE DAMAGE:
Bark blown off
hardwood trees.
Most portions of
houses destroyed.

4

166–200 mph
(267–322km/h)

DEVASTATING DAMAGE:
Complete destruction
of well-built homes
and sections of school
buildings.

Deadly EF-5s

Supertwisters are destructive tornadoes with
winds of 200 mph (322km/h) or faster. They
cause 67 percent of the U.S. tornado deaths.

5

More than
200 mph
(322km/h)

**INCREDIBLE
DAMAGE:**
Significant destruction
to mid- and high-rise
buildings.

Tornadoes to Remember: Four Devastating Twisters

Living through a twister isn't something tornado survivors ever forget. The storms documented in the following pages are some of the most powerful, devastating, and destructive tornadoes on record.

The Tri-State Tornado

Where: Eastern Missouri, southern Illinois, and southwestern Indiana
When: March 18, 1925 • **What:** F-5 • **How Bad:** 695 dead; 2,027 injured

March 18, 1925, was a Wednesday. Students looked out from classroom windows, farmers stopped and stared in fields, and mothers paused while hanging laundry—the dark, threatening sky had caught everyone's attention. Around 1:00 p.m., trees started snapping near Ellington, Missouri. Strong storms had spawned a giant wedge tornado. For the next 3½ hours, the twister plowed through twenty towns in three states.

When it was over, the Tri-State Tornado had left a record-breaking path of pain and ruin. Murphysboro, Illinois, lost 234 citizens. The town-eating tornado destroyed some 15,000 homes along its track through small mining and farming communities. A St. Louis newspaper wrote that "the air was filled with 10,000 things. Boards, poles, cans, garments, stoves, whole sides of the little frame houses, in some cases the houses themselves, were picked up and smashed to earth. And living beings, too. A baby was blown from its mother's arms. A cow, picked up by the wind, was hurled into the village restaurant."

The Tri-State Tornado caused major destruction in the town of West Frankfort, Illinois.

Record-breaking Killer

The Tri-State Tornado is the deadliest in U.S. history.

Track of Terror

The Tri-State Tornado plowed the longest track of destruction of any in the United States.

A DEADLY PATH

The monster tornado covered 219 miles (352km) at record-breaking travel speeds (marked on map). Its maximum speed of 73 mph (117km/h) makes the Tri-State the fastest moving tornado ever. Modern meteorologists believe there might have been more than one tornado, however.

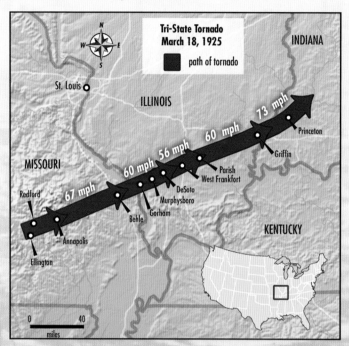

I WAS THERE!

Surviving at School

The Tri-State Tornado destroyed every single building in Gorham, Illinois—including the small school. A schoolgirl who survived described what happened when the twister hit the school. She said, "The walls seemed to fall in, all around us. Then the floor at one end of the building gave way. We all slipped or slid in that direction. If it hadn't been for the seats it would have been like sliding down a cellar door. I can't tell you what happened then. I can't describe it. I can't bear to think about it. Children all around me...cried and screamed. It was something awful. I had to close my eyes..." Seven students died that day in Gorham. More than sixty other students died at schools in DeSoto and Murphysboro. Most were killed by tumbling brick walls.

The Longfellow School in Murphysboro, Illinois, shown here, was one of several schools that suffered major damage in the Tri-State Tornado.

The Super Outbreak

Where: 13 midwestern and southern states • **When:** April 3–4, 1974
What: 148 tornadoes from F-0 to F-5 • **How Bad:** 330 dead; 5,484 injured

• •

On April 3, 1974, forecasters knew the United States was in for some severe storms. They'd issued 28 severe weather watches and 150 tornado warnings across much of the eastern half of the United States. However, no one had any idea how bad it'd get. By 2:00 p.m., tornadoes were hitting Tennessee and Georgia. Minutes later twisters touched down in Illinois and Indiana. And that was just the beginning. By the time the storms stopped early the next morning, 148 tornadoes had struck 13 states.

Alabama, Kentucky, and Ohio were especially hard hit. One supertwister tore up the town of Xenia, Ohio. It grew into an F-5 after three separate tornadoes combined. The Xenia supertwister trashed 1,000 homes and killed 34 people. "There's never been anything like it before, as far as we know, or since," says meteorologist Joseph Shaefer. "It was a once-in-a-century event, and probably rarer than that."

Unlucky April

The storms that hit in April of 1974 made up the largest and worst tornado outbreak in U.S. history.

A WIDESPREAD PATH

These are the tracks of the 148 tornadoes that hit during the 16-hour outbreak. The damage path covered more than 2,500 miles (4,023km).

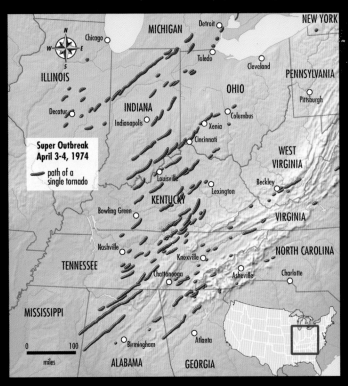

I WAS THERE!
A Deafening Wind

Jeff Louderback was only five years old in 1974, but as he looked out the window of his home in Xenia, Ohio, he knew what he was seeing. A giant, wide tornado was coming toward his house.

"Mom and Dad covered me, shielding my body from flying bricks and shattered glass," Louderback recalled twenty-five years later. "The deafening wind sounded like a team of fighter jets. I saw bedroom doors slamming against the wall before flying off their hinges. The roof ripped off, and the walls around us crumbled." The Louderback family survived the F-5 tornado that hit Xenia that day. Their house did not. Jeff's mom Rebecca Louderback remembers seeing their destroyed neighborhood after the storm. "It was probably very similar to the aftermath of a bomb," she said. "It was eerily quiet. Then you started to hear children crying."

Xenia residents banded together to help neighbors, like the Louderback family, whose homes were destroyed by the 1974 tornado. In this photograph, one resident cleans up the wreckage.

Oklahoma City Outbreak

Where: Central Oklahoma • **When:** May 3, 1999
What: 74 tornadoes from F-0 to F-5
How Bad: 46 dead; 800 injured

What could make an outbreak of seventy-four tornadoes across central Oklahoma worse? An F-5 supertwister tornado hitting the densely populated suburbs of Oklahoma City.

May 3, 1999, started out hot and muggy. As the day went on, weather forecasters watched supercell thunderstorms grow. By late afternoon, the storms had started to spit out tornadoes—one after another after another. Up to four were on the ground at the same time! The strongest one swirled along a 38-mile (61km) track of total devastation for more than an hour. It ravaged south Oklahoma City and the suburbs of Bridge Creek and Moore.

Once the skies cleared, survivors climbed out of more than eight thousand damaged or ruined homes. Hundreds of lives were saved in the area, thanks to good forecasting. Residents had fifteen to thirty minutes or more of warning before twisters hit their neighborhoods. Meteorologists and news stations tracked the storms with radar and even helicopters. Radios and televisions alerted those in the storm's path to move underground, if possible. Few homes survive supertwister F-5 winds.

Pricey Twister

Nearly $1.5 billion in damage makes the Oklahoma Tornado outbreak of 1999 one of the top five costliest U.S. tornadoes of all time.

A COSTLY PATH

The strongest F-5 twister luckily missed downtown Oklahoma City, but it trashed the suburbs of Bridge Creek and Moore.

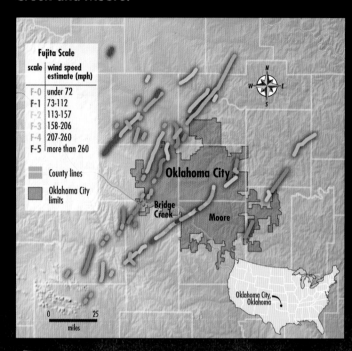

Fujita Scale	
scale	wind speed estimate (mph)
F-0	under 72
F-1	73-112
F-2	113-157
F-3	158-206
F-4	207-260
F-5	more than 260

County lines

Oklahoma City limits

Oklahoma City

Bridge Creek

Moore

0 25
miles

Oklahoma City, Oklahoma

Record-setting Winds

Weather radar clocked the Bridge Creek F-5 tornado's winds at 301 mph (484km/h)—the fastest ever recorded.

I WAS THERE!

Houses Crack Apart

Like many Oklahomans on May 3, 1999, Mary and Tom Chase first saw the tornado on TV. "We were able to follow the whole thing on television," explained Tom Chase. "Oh, we had plenty of warning, plenty." So, it wasn't much of a surprise when the supertwister showed up in their Moore neighborhood. "Finally, we could hear it outside," said Chase. "I walked out on the front porch and there it was, black and twirling, all this debris spinning up in the sky."

The couple scurried down into their underground shelter. As the supertwister passed over them, the whole shelter shook and throbbed like a sore tooth. "There was one big crack and the house was gone above us. We heard it coming apart. Just crack, and it was gone," said Chase. "It was an awesome thing." The Chase's home was completely destroyed. "But we'll build the house back. You can't build people back." Sometimes, people feel lucky just to survive.

A powerful tornado from the May 3rd outbreak destroyed this truck and left its remains tangled in a tree.

31

A DISASTROUS PATH

The tornado that leveled Greensburg plowed a 1.7-mile wide (2.7km) path—as wide as the entire town.

Area of tornado
County Lines

Greensburg

9:59 PM
9:55 PM
9:39 PM
9:34 PM
9:12 PM
9:08 PM
9:00 PM

Greensburg, Kansas

0   10
miles

Infamous First

The Greensburg Tornado was the first EF-5 rated twister.

I WAS THERE!
Four Minutes That Seemed Like a Lifetime

Megan Gardiner was a teenager looking forward to a Friday night with friends on May 4, 2007. When tornado warning sirens starting wailing, she headed home instead and joined her family and neighbors in the basement. Soon hail the size of golf balls starting pounding the house. Megan crouched down by a sofa, grabbing a pillow and blanket for protection as the wind picked up and the lights went out. "All of a sudden my ears started to pop really bad," remembered Megan. "I mean this was worse than going in a plane or diving deep under the water." Then the windows exploded. The tornado was over them. "I heard the walls tearing and ripping off into pieces. Then something fell on my left shoulder and I had my head covered with my hands, like the drills we do in school . . . The sound was like a jet engine going right over us, about to take off. Just hearing the house rip into shreds

was horrible. . . . What seemed like a lifetime finally came to an end. Then I started to yell, 'Is everyone okay?' . . . I turned and saw the roof was covering my feet."

It took Megan and her family a half hour to crawl out of the rubble that was once their home. "I mean, again, there are no words to describe the devastation we saw. It's nothing like the pictures and TV. In real life it's 100 times worse because you can see everything just shredded and ripped into pieces." But the tornado didn't end that night for Megan. Weeks later Megan was still having nightmares about the storm. Her parents suggested writing about it, which she did—and that helped. "I didn't have to hold everything in anymore," Megan said. "May 4 changed 1,500 people's lives when the EF-5 tornado came through," wrote Megan. "I was one of them."

The Greensburg Tornado

Where: Greensburg, Kansas • **When:** May 4, 2007
What: EF-5 • **How Bad:** 12 dead; 60 injured

A single twister can turn a farm town into a ghost town. On the morning of May 4, 2007, Greensburg, Kansas, was home to 1,500 people. That night, a giant wedge tornado bulldozed the whole town. Meteorologists had given residents a rare amount of advanced warning. Tornado emergency warning sirens rang out a full twenty minutes ahead of the twister. This warning gave residents time to seek underground shelter—and saved hundreds of lives. But the town was flattened.

An unbelievable 95 percent of buildings in Greensburg were damaged. Trucks were tossed atop piles of splintered homes. Trees stripped of their bark bled sap. The town had to be evacuated and the highway routed around it. "All my downtown is gone," said Greensburg city manager Steve Hewitt. "My home is gone. My staff's homes are gone. . . . It's going to be tough."

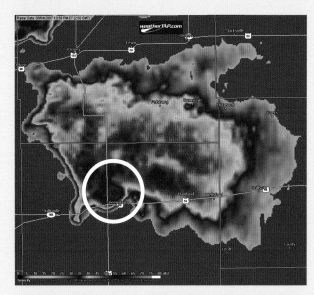

Radar images show the severity of storms and can help scientists predict the likelihood of a tornado. In this case, the Greensburg tornado was so large and had so much debris whirling in its winds that the actual tornado (circled) can be seen on the radar image.

BEFORE

AFTER

Aerial photographs of Greensburg, Kansas, before and after a tornado struck in 2007.

Tornadoes are equal opportunity destroyers. These powerful wind storms happen all over the world. A tornado plowed across the border of southern Argentina and Brazil in 2009, shredding hundreds of houses and killing fourteen people. Killer tornadoes also sometimes strike India, Russia, South Africa, China, and Canada.

While the U.S. gets most of the strongest twisters, other regions suffer more loss of life. The south Asian country of Bangladesh bears the heaviest burden. Tornadoes there often leave hundreds dead. During the past four decades twisters have killed more than 5,000 Bangladeshis. The world's deadliest tornado ever happened in Bangladesh in 1989. The Daultipur-Salturia Tornado (named after the two cities it flattened) harmed an unbelievable number of people. The storm killed 1,300; injured 12,000; and left 80,000 people homeless. It's a world record that will hopefully never be broken.

In Harm's Way

The south Asian country of Bangladesh is only the size of Wisconsin, but 150 million people live there. That's half the entire U.S. population.

Global Tornadoes

This astonishing photograph captures four waterspout tornadoes over a portion of the Adriatic Sea off the coast of Albania.

Storm Scientists in Action

Running Down the Storm

Golden grain fields glow in the late afternoon Texas sun. The picture isn't so pretty overhead, though. Black clouds tumble and rumble. Lightning slams the ground nearby, followed by bone-rattling thunder. Minivans, trucks, and wind-blown people wait next to the farm fields along the road. They scan the stormy sky for signs of a twister. Then a voice comes over their radios. It's meteorologist Josh Wurman saying, "There's now a stronger tornado developing." It's just a mile up the road—time to go!

The storm chasers jump into their vehicles and race off—toward the twister! Their goal is to get close to the tornado, usually between 1/2 to 3 miles away (0.8 to 5km). After a bit of back and forth on the country roads, a tornado is spotted. "There it is," one driver yells. The twister is thin, ropy, and white. Its top bends over like an elbow.

Wurman's team is instantly at work collecting weather information. They track the tornado's direction and measure wind speeds of 139 mph (224km/h). Then all of sudden, the twister turns. "It is coming right at us," warns Wurman. Chasers in a parked pickup truck are too close to get out of the way! They just sit tight and hope for the best. The tornado's wind rocks the truck, pulling the windshield wipers off as debris swirls around them. A metal barrel flies past them at 100 mph (161km/h)—and barely misses them. Then, it's over. "Everybody okay? Everyone all right?" they ask each other. Incredibly, everyone answers, "Yes."

Some people chase tornadoes for the thrill. Wurman's team put themselves in harm's way for science. There are thousands of supercell thunder-storms a year. But "only about 5 percent of them make severe tornadoes—the ones that kill people," says Wurman. Predicting exactly which supercell is going to kick out a killer tornado—and when—isn't yet possible for scientists. "There's still a lot we need to learn."

Josh Wurman searches the skies.

Tornado Forecasting 101

How do meteorologists forecast tornadoes?
A twister's short life makes it tough. Tornadoes often appear and disappear in seconds. However, scientists *can* track and forecast the severe thunderstorms that make tornadoes. Meteorologists gather weather information such as temperature, pressure, and wind speed and direction through satellite pictures, weather balloons, and radar. Computers crunch all the numbers and help forecasters predict where thunderstorms might form over the next twelve to forty-eight hours.

Once a severe thunderstorm appears, Doppler radar watches for a tornado-making mesocyclone inside it. A tell-tale "hook echo" on radar shows where a tornado might spin up. The problem is that the storm has to be close to a radar tower for a hook echo to show. If it's too far way, what's inside the storm is invisible. Josh Wurman got tired of waiting for thunderstorms to happen close enough to radar towers to be able to study them. So, ten years ago he invented a way to take the radar to the storm instead.

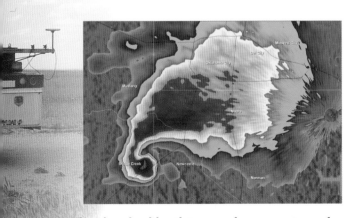

A hook echo like this one shows up in radar images of a rotating thunderstorm that may kick out a tornado. Green is light rain, yellow is heavy rain, and red is pouring rain. In a rotating supercell, rain wraps around this circulation and creates the hook shape.

Spotting Storms with Radar

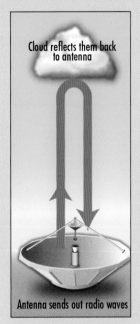

Cloud reflects them back to antenna

Antenna sends out radio waves

Radar is an important tool for storm chasers. How does radar work? An antenna sends out radio waves. When those waves hit raindrops, snowflakes, hail, or other stuff in the air the radio waves bounce back to the antenna. It works like sounds bouncing back in an echo. The patterns of bounced back radio waves are electronically made into a picture that shows where it's raining or snowing.

Newer Doppler radar can also show wind speeds and direction. How? It's like the change in sound of a passing ambulance's siren or the honking of a car horn. The sound changes because its frequency changes, stretching out as it gets farther away from you. Doppler radar measures the frequency changes of the radio waves it sends out. The changes tell the Doppler radar if the rain is moving away or toward its antennae—and which way and how fast it's moving.

Radar has made a huge difference in forecasting tornadoes—and has saved countless lives. The average warning time for a tornado is now around fourteen minutes. That's often enough time to get to a safe place.

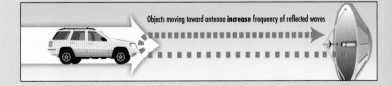

Objects moving toward antenna **increase** frequency of reflected waves

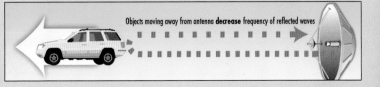

Objects moving away from antenna **decrease** frequency of reflected waves

Chasing Down Data

Josh Wurman's invention is called Doppler On Wheels, or DOW for short. DOWs are basically "trucks with big antennae on the back," explains Wurman. The mobile Doppler radar is custom built to take bumpy rides. DOWs also have a big cab behind the driver. It's full of radios and computers that track storms and record the radar's measurements. This is where Wurman sits and tracks tornadoes. A satellite dish on top of the truck sends and receives wireless Internet data, television signals, and weather radio bulletins. It's quite a vehicle!

A DOW's million-dollar equipment package can see and record what's inside a storm. Because they're mobile, DOWs can get close to a tornado. Wurman was able to get within a mile of a supertwister that killed forty people in Oklahoma in 1999 (see page 30–31). His DOW recorded the fastest tornado winds ever—301 mph (484km/h).

Wurman's DOWs have chased and scanned more than one hundred twisters. "Our goal is to get as complete a picture of the tornado as we can," he explains. "The radar enables us to take multiple slices through the tornado every ten seconds to a minute and make 3-D images of the outside and the inside of the tornado." Knowing a tornado's direction, intensity, and wind speed makes warnings more accurate and detailed. Knowing where a tornado's going and how strong it is can help save lives.

Josh Wurman and his team have seen a lot— doors flying off trucks, bits of houses falling from the sky, and enough hail to fill a swimming pool. But he insists, "It's safer than you think. We've got radar and so we know when to get out of the way."

A Doppler On Wheels unit tracks a tornado near Attica, Kansas.

Talk Like a Tornado Chaser

anvil zits: Frequent lightning within a thunderstorm cloud, which is also called an anvil cloud.

blue watch: Severe thunderstorm watch.

bust: Storm watch that only delivers a moderate amount of stormy weather.

core punching: Driving through the part of the storm with the heaviest rain and hail—the core.

gunge: Stuff that makes it harder to see a storm, like fog, haze, rain, low clouds, and so on.

red watch or red box: Tornado watch.

storm chaser: Someone who hunts for and follows storms for research, photography, or news reporting.

storm spotter: On-the-ground volunteer reporter for the National Weather Service. (Want to be one? Go to www.skywarn.org.)

I WAS THERE!
Playing Chicken with an F-4

Storm chaser Tim Samaras was scanning the skies near Manchester, South Dakota, on June 24, 2003, when a big one showed up. An F-4 tornado with 200 mph (322km/h) winds began plowing across the lonely farm country. Samaras and his crew flew into action. They were there to put tornado-measuring probes into the path of twisters. Samaras designed the flying saucer–shaped probes, packed with cameras and weather measuring instruments. The tricky part is placing them in the tornado's path—and getting out of the way safely.

Samaras daringly drove to about 100 yards (91m) ahead of the tornado to set the last probe onto the ground. "That's the closest I've been to a violent tornado," recalled Samaras. "And I have no desire to ever be that close again." The powerful tornado tore across where Samaras had been working just 60 seconds later. "Debris was flying overhead, telephone poles were snapped and flung 300 yards (274m) through the air, roads ripped from the ground, and the town of Manchester literally sucked into the clouds," Samaras reported. Thankfully, no one was hurt—and the probe survived, too!

On June 11, 2005, cameras inside storm chaser Tim Samaras's probes captured video of the inside of a tornado as it passed overhead. This 2006 photograph shows Samaras with one of his red flying saucer-shaped probes.

Virtual Twisters

While chasing tornadoes is exciting, it's a tough way to collect information. Not only is reaching a storm in time hard to do, but also once a tornado is spotted, it's often over in an instant. What can slow down a tornado so it can be studied in more detail? A supercomputer.

Scientists can simulate 3-D tornadoes on supercomputers. They create a virtual thunderstorm by plugging in weather information such as wind speeds, humidity, and temperature. Once set into motion, the simulated storm grows on its own—and creates a tornado! "It's a fairly amazing thing," agrees meteorologist Lou Wicker. He's simulated tornadoes on computers over many years.

Watching virtual tornadoes being born is mind-blowing. However, Wicker isn't convinced that the virtual tornadoes are born in the same way a Kansas twister is. Any computer simulation is only as good as the information fed into it—and good weather information on tornadoes is hard to get. Wicker is working on using real tornado-making thunderstorm radar to create virtual thunderstorms. Then he'll be able to compare the virtual twister to the real tornado that storm chasers measured.

This virtual supercomputer simulation of a tornado crunches so much data that it takes more than a week to run. The orange lines are rising air, the blue are falling air, and the swaying cones show wind speed and direction on the ground.

Tornado Safety

Tornadoes are pretty scary. Being prepared can help keep you safe if a twister visits your neighborhood someday. Learn what the different weather alerts mean, make a plan, and practice it!

Stay Alert! Be Warned!

Weather Alert	What It Means	What to Do
TORNADO WATCH	Tornadoes are possible in your area. Remain alert for approaching storms.	• Keep the TV or radio on for updates. Set the alarm switch on a weather radio if you have one. • Know where you can take shelter, if needed. (See "Give Me Shelter.") • Tell others there's a tornado watch.
TORNADO WARNING	A tornado has been sighted or indicated by weather radar. Take shelter now.	This depends on where you are. (See "Give Me Shelter.")
TORNADO EMERGENCY	A large, violent tornado is expected to hit a populated area.	Seek serious shelter—below ground or in a tornado shelter—if possible.

Give Me Shelter

"Taking shelter" is good advice, but what does that mean exactly? It depends on where you are.

If you're in a building or house,

- Go to a basement, if possible. If not, go to a room on the lowest floor in the middle of the building—a bathroom, closet, hallway, or under a stairway. Stay away from windows! Stay out of elevators!
- Crawl under a sturdy piece of furniture or into a bathtub.
- Cover yourself with a mattress or blanket, if possible. If not, crouch low, head down, and protect the back of your head with your arms.

If you're in a car,

- Park and go to a building, if there's time.
- Tornado on its way? The driver should quickly park the car out of traffic so that everyone can get out of and away from the car.
- Don't hide under a bridge or highway overpass. It's dangerous.

If you're outdoors,

- Find a culvert (very large pipe), ditch, or cave, and crawl in. The lower the better!
- Get away from trees or cars that might be blown at you.
- Lie flat and face down. Cover your head.

- **Don't** open windows. It's a myth that doing that keeps a house from exploding. You could be hit with flying glass while doing it.
- **Do** get to the lowest place possible. Tornado winds are weaker near the ground.

- **Don't** stay in a mobile home, camper, van, or car. It's not safe.
- **Do** protect your head! Cover it with whatever you can, even your arms.

Keep an Eye on the Sky!

Radar and storm spotters can't catch every tornado. While a funnel-shaped twister is easy to spot, a tornado hidden by rain or at night is not. Here are some signs a twister may be near:

- Hail or heavy rain falls and then there's either dead calm or a fast shift in the wind. Many tornadoes can't be seen because they're surrounded by rain.
- There's a loud roar or rumbling sound that doesn't fade in a few seconds, like thunder would.
- The bottom of the thunderstorm cloud is spinning quickly.
- There's whirling dust or debris on the ground under a thunderstorm cloud. Sometimes a tornado's funnel is invisible.
- Power lines snapping can mean a tornado. At night, they'll look like small, bright, blue-green-to-white flashes near the ground below a thunderstorm. Lightning is more silvery and flashes up in the clouds.

Tornado Activity: Get It Together

The best time to figure out what to do during a tornado is before the storm starts! Here's how to get ready:

1. **Make a family plan—and practice it.**
   - **Know where to go!** Decide where your tornado shelter will be—the basement, a neighbor's cellar, the downstairs bathroom, and so on.
   - **Tornado Watch List.** Make a list of what to get together during a tornado watch, in case it becomes a warning and you have to seek shelter. (Pets, blankets, shoes, etc.)
   - **Tornado Drill!** Practice going to that shelter (as if there were a real tornado), wearing sturdy shoes, and taking whatever is on your list.

2. **Put together a storm survival kit:** highway map of your area (so you know where the tornado is from weather bulletins), flashlight or light sticks (not candles), battery or crank-powered radio or weather radio, fire extinguisher, pocket tool or knife, first aid kit, and bottles of water.

3. **Post your Tornado Watch List somewhere easy to see.**

FEARSOME and Mysterious Storms

With the fastest winds on Earth, tornadoes are the planet's most violent storms. These short-lived bursts of town-trashing, whirling wind are thankfully rare. However, tornadoes come from common thunderstorms. It's still a modern meteorological mystery why some thunderstorms spin out twisters and other don't. Storm-chasing scientists are working hard to uncover twister secrets. Their work improves tornado forecasting, giving people in a tornado's path more time to safely seek shelter and save their lives. Want to keep learning about tornadoes? Flip up this page to Find Out More!

BIBLIOGRAPHY

Carson, Mary Kay. *Weather Projects for Young Scientists*. Chicago: Chicago Review Press, 2007.

Edwards, Roger. "The Online Tornado FAQ," NOAA/NWS: Storm Prediction Center. http://www.spc.ncep.noaa.gov/faq/tornado/index.html.

Ezard, John. "Blown away." *The Guardian*, May 6, 1999.

"A Severe Weather Primer: Questions and Answers about TORNADOES." National Severe Storms Laboratory (NSSL). www.nssl.noaa.gov/primer/tornado/tor_basics.html.

Tornado Project Online. http://www.tornadoproject.com.

"Tornadoes." University of Illinois WW2010. http://ww2010.atmos.uiuc.edu/%28Gh%29/guides/mtr/svr/torn/home.rxml.

Williams, Jack. *The Weather Book: An Easy-to-Understand Guide to the US's Weather*. New York: Vintage, 1997.

SOURCE NOTES

PAGE 16: "We don't really . . . a leading candidate,": *Hunt for the Supertwister,* DVD, directed by Thomas Lucas (Boston, MA: WGBH Educational Foundation 2004).

PAGE 16: "That RFD has . . . have right now,": *Hunt for the Supertwister,* DVD, directed by Thomas Lucas (Boston, MA: WGBH Educational Foundation 2004).

PAGE 20: "You might have . . . soon to say.": Roger Edwards of Storm Prediction Center, author of "Will Global Warming Cause More Tornadoes?," e-mail correspondence with author, August 15, 2007.

PAGE 20: "You might have . . . to have tornadoes.": Dr. Louis Wicker, research scientist, National Severe Storms Laboratory, telephone interview with the author, August 16, 2007.

PAGE 20: "For all its . . . to ever occur.": Roger Edwards of Storm Prediction Center, author of "Will Global Warming Cause More Tornadoes?," e-mail correspondence with author, August 15, 2007.

PAGE 20: "It's not much . . . to global climate,": Roger Edwards of Storm Prediction Center, author of "Will Global Warming Cause More Tornadoes?," e-mail correspondence with author, August 15, 2007.

PAGE 26: "the air was filled . . . the village restaurant.": Peter S. Felknor, *The Tri-State Tornado: The Story of America's Greatest Tornado Disaster,* (Lincoln, NE: iUniverse, 2004).

PAGE 27: "There's never been . . . rarer than that.": John Galvin, "Super Tornado Outbreak: Miss. and Ohio River Valleys, April 1974," *Popular Mechanics,* July 31, 2007, www.popularmechanics.com/science/worst_case_scenarios/4219870.html.

PAGE 28: "Mom and Dad . . . around us crumbled.": John Galvin, "Super Tornado Outbreak: Miss. and Ohio River Valleys, April 1974," *Popular Mechanics,* July 31, 2007, www.popularmechanics.com/science/worst_case_scenarios/4219870.html.

PAGE 28: "It was probably . . . hear children crying.": Associated Press, "Community recalls terror of tornado at anniversary '74 twister among nation's worst,". *Florida Times Union*, April 4, 1999.

PAGE 29: "The walls seemed . . . close my eyes . . .": Peter S. Felknor, *The Tri-State Tornado: The Story of America's Greatest Tornado Disaster* (Lincoln, NE: iUniverse, 2004).

PAGE 31: "We were able . . . it was gone.": Rick Lyman, "Residents Watched on TV As the Tornadoes Neared," *New York Times*, May 6, 1999.

PAGE 31: "It was an awesome . . . build people back,": John Ezard, "Blown away," *The Guardian*, May 6, 1999.

PAGE 33: "All my downtown . . . to be tough,": Peter Slevin, "At Least 9 Dead After Tornado Ravages Kansas Town," *Washington Post*, May 6, 2007.

PAGE 34: "All of a sudden . . . one of them.": Megan Gardiner, "Megan Gardiner's account of surviving the Greensburg tornado," *The Wichita Eagle*, May 14, 2009, http://www.kansas.com/greensburg/story/792622.html.

PAGE 35: "Nearly 700 people . . . a mass grave.": Reuters, "Bangladesh tornado area short on food," *Chicago Tribune*, May, 2, 1989.

PAGE 36: "I saw the . . . I do not know.": "Storms Bring Death, Damage as Drought End in Bangladesh," *Seattle Times,* April 27, 1989.

PAGE 38: "There's now a stronger tornado developing.": *National Geographic: Tornado Intercept*

TORNADO WATCHER WORDS TO KNOW

ATMOSPHERE the blanket of air that surrounds Earth and lies between its land or oceans and outer space

DOPPLER RADAR a type of radar that uses radio frequency changes to measure wind speed and direction

DOWNDRAFT downward moving air

DRY LINE the boundary between a moist air mass and a dry air mass

FRONT the boundary between two different air masses

MESOCYCLONE the vertical spinning air inside a supercell thunderstorm

METEOROLOGIST a scientist who studies weather

RADAR short for RAdio Detecting And Ranging, it's a technology for detecting distant objects, including rain, clouds, and storms

REAR FLANK DOWNDRAFT (RFD) a strong downdraft of air on the backside of a thunderstorm

SEVERE THUNDERSTORM a thunderstorm with winds faster than 58 mph (93km/h), hail larger than ¾-inch (2cm) across, or tornadoes

SUPERCELL a large thunderstorm with a mesocyclone inside it

TORNADO a violently rotating column of air coming down from a thunderstorm cloud and in contact with the ground

UPDRAFT upward moving air

VORTEX spinning air or water

WALL CLOUD a part of a thunderstorm cloud that hangs down and spins and sometimes produces tornadoes

WIND SHEAR the difference in wind speed and/or direction between two short distances

DVD, produced and written by Lawrence Cumbo (National Geographic Video, 2006).

PAGE 38: "There it is,": *National Geographic: Tornado Intercept*, DVD, produced and written by Lawrence Cumbo (National Geographic Video, 2006).

PAGE 38: "It is coming . . . yes.": *National Geographic: Tornado Intercept*, DVD, produced and written by Lawrence Cumbo (National Geographic Video, 2006).

PAGE 38: "only about 5 percent . . . need to learn.": Interview with Josh Wurman on *Whad'Ya Know?*, March 31, 2007, http://www.notmuch.com/Show/Archive.pl?s_id=449.

PAGE 39: "We didn't have Doppler radar fifteen or twenty years ago,": Dr. Louis Wicker, research scientist, National Severe Storms Laboratory, telephone with interview with the author, August 16, 2007.

PAGE 40: "trucks with big antennae on the back,": Interview with Josh Wurman on *Whad'Ya Know?*, March 31, 2007, http://www.notmuch.com/Show/Archive.pl?s_id=449.

PAGE 40: "Our goal is . . . of the tornado.": Stefan Lovgren, "Tornado Intercept Offers Rare Peek at a Twister Touchdown," *National Geographic News*, December 16, 2005.

PAGE 40: "It's safer than . . . get out the way.": Interview with Josh Wurman on *Whad'Ya Know?*, March 31, 2007, http://www.notmuch.com/Show/Archive.pl?s_id=449.

PAGE 41: "That's the closest . . . into the clouds,: Tim Samaras, "Tim's Biography," ThunderChase.com, http://thunderchase.com/content/view/14/32/.

PAGE 42: "It's a fairly amazing thing,": Dr. Louis Wicker, research scientist, National Severe Storms Laboratory, telephone interview with the author, August 16, 2007.

FIND OUT MORE
WEB SITES TO VISIT
FEMA for Kids
www.fema.gov/kids/tornado.htm
The Federal Emergency Management Agency's site for kids about tornadoes and storm safety. Get in the know and get ready!

The Online Tornado FAQ
www.spc.ncep.noaa.gov/faq/tornado/
The Storm Prediction Center has all the answers, plus information and links about storm chasers and storm spotters.

Tornado Chaser Kids
www.tornadochaser.com/2000projects.htm
Fun projects to do as well as storm information.

Hunt for the Supertwister
www.pbs.org/wgbh/nova/tornado/
This NOVA Web site has lots of tornado tracking and forecasting information as well as a Rate Tornado Damage interactive.

Climate Change Kids Site
www.epa.gov/climatechange/kids/
Find out more about climate change—and what to do about it—at this Environmental Protection Agency Web site.

DVDS TO WATCH
Mega Disasters: "Tornado Alley" (History Channel) (DVD, 2009).
National Geographic: *Tornado Intercept* (DVD, 2006).
Storm Chasers (Discovery Channel) (DVD, 2008).

BOOKS TO READ
Storm Scientist: Careers Chasing Severe Weather by Timothy R. Gaffney (Enslow, 2009).
Tornadoes by Michael Woods (Lerner, 2007).
Tornadoes: The Science Behind Terrible Twisters by Alvin Silverstein (Enslow, 2009).

INDEX